ANGELIQ

WORTH
FIGHTING
FOR

A SURVIVOR'S STORY

Worth Fighting For

I dedicate this book to the loving memory of my dad William Barr, my aunt Rosa Lee Suber and my nephew Gerrod Lucas; I love and miss you all everyday.

ACKNOWLEDGMENTS

To my mother Cathryn Barr, thank you for your love and support. You have always supported my dreams. Thank you for allowing me to be your favorite daughter.

To my sisters: Felicia, Vanessa (Shang), Bunny and Denise, there aren't enough words to express how much I love you and appreciate you.

To T.J., Shannon, Denise, Deidra, Shanice, Kee, Des'Ree, Laila- Catherine, Caleb, Keith and Kamaria and the kids and Keya, I love you all so much.

To Carroll W. Gibbs, you have been my safe space since day one. We have been through a lot together, thank you for everything, I love you.

To my pastor, Apostle Ronald L. Demery, Jr. and Lady LaShawn Demery, thank you both for always supporting my family and I. The love you have shown us makes us family, period.

ACKNOWLEDGMENTS

To Lewis and Sharon Johnson, thank you both for your love and support. I could not have done this without the both of you.

To my aunt Tina and uncle Johnathan Lamb, thank you for the rides to my appointments and for the many laughs. To uncle Bishop Larry and aunt Anita Frazier, thank you for everything.

To Bishop Aaron and Lady Isabel Pollard, thank you for taking such great care of me.

Thank you to everyone who took the time to visit me, call me, to check in on me, or just to come sit with me. I appreciate everything.

Thank you Jesus for giving me the patience to wait on you when everyone was telling me, "you need to write a book", not knowing or understanding I had to deal with the trauma of being hours away from dying and the grief of seeing my dad slowly decline while still dealing with my unresolved issues. Thank you to those that prayed for me and those that prayed against me. God is forever fighting for me.

PROLOGUE

Worth Fighting For recounts many of my own personal life experiences. I wrote this book to encourage someone that God is always fighting for them, that we are in a fixed fight and that no matter what we go through in life, we just have to go through the process because in the end, WE WIN. Thank you Bishop Neil and Pastor Dee Gross for always reminding me that "WE WIN".

~ Althea Angelique Barr

TESTIMONIAL

"I want to say it was in February of the transplant year when we were informed that Angel was admitted into George Washington Hospital. I can't remember if we, or specifically I, was told how critical her health had become, or if I refused or didn't want to believe the report was "bad". Nevertheless, my husband Darrell and I decided that we were going to travel from Philly to see Angel the following weekend. As the week went on, it was being reported a possible snow storm could hit the region on that Saturday. Each day, the reports changed the storm into a significant event so by Thursday and definitely by Friday, I wondered if we were going to have to postpone the trip. It was on Friday that Darrell confirmed we were going to see Angel. We planned on leaving for D.C. mid to late Saturday morning. I was thinking to myself Darrell may have wanted a late start, so we could be on the other side of the storm once it hit the area. Saturday morning arrived and it hadn't started to snow in or around the Philly area. After being on the road for about a half an hour, so far, so good. Then, after about another half an hour or so of traveling, we began to see the first flakes of the storm. Apparently, the storm was moving South to North, so we were traveling into the storm. Traffic was moving at a steady pace as those on the road were driving with caution.

The further we traveled down I-95 South, the heavier the snow got. Once we made it to Baltimore and its tunnel, I thought we should make it to the hospital to see my sister in good time, in spite of the storm. Then, traffic came to a standstill as we continued traveling toward Columbia, MD. This stretch of I-95 was completely covered with snow, with no evidence of a snowplow coming through to clear the roads. Therefore, Darrell decided to exit off this major highway onto Route 32. Half way onto the exit ramp, the unexpected happened: the jeep began to slide. Although Darrell was maneuvering the wheel, the rule of "steering in the direction of the skid until you regain traction" failed, and the jeep slid into a ditch.

I may have closed my eyes for a moment as I called on Jesus to myself. The jeep was now positioned on a slant toward the passenger's side. When I checked on the kids, they appeared unfazed during this mishap. I thanked God no one was hurt and there was little to no damage to the Trailblazer. It had to be at least an hour (or two) before we were rescued by a tow truck that transported us to either the nearest gas station or rest stop. We then continued on our journey.

After five to six hours, God's protection allowed us to arrive at George Washington Hospital to see our sister, aunt and godmother. Our journey was delayed but not denied. It wasn't until after Angel's one year transplant anniversary that she was told of the details of our trip on that Saturday in February: A journey because of love."

~ Denise Gibbs

TESTIMONIAL

"It was a Sunday morning when Bishop Ronald L. Demery, Jr. asked everyone to pray for Angel because she was very sick and the doctors said there was nothing else they could do for her. The church immediately went into prayer for Angel and the Barr family. The following week or so, Bishop asked for more prayers because Angel was having transplant surgery. I believed God was going to bring Angel back to us so I continued to pray. Angel is a very valuable person in my life. I can talk to her and get advice from her. When I had my kidney transplant years after she did, there was so much I didn't understand but she was right there to comfort and enlighten me. She would always say, "God has given us a second chance at life, so we have to live our lives to the glory of God everyday"."

~ Kerri "KK" Boyd

FOREWORD

I have known Angel for well over 40 years. The warm, positive and generous lady that you will come to appreciate through "Worth Fighting For" will not only encourage you to face life's challenges, but it will also add to your level of faith. Angel has approached each day with a smile, high energy and hard work. She does not simply talk the talk - she walks the walk!

Upon reading this book, I discovered a personal initiate journey of a fighter. It reminds me of the adage that everyone has a story to tell. Her story of overcoming difficulties and not allowing circumstances to dictate your outlook on life is a must read for both young and old. This book is not just another religious story, but gives practical insights into how to navigate various storms of life. Angel put a real face on the description of a fighter!!!

I hope this book is widely circulated and taken to heart not only by Christians, but even more importantly by those who may find themselves in a battle. Then I believe they will share in the possibility that Life is Worth Fighting For!!

~ Bishop M.K. Smith

TABLE OF CONTENTS

IN THE BEGINNING | 13

IN THE NEIGHBORHOOD | 17

THE BIG MOVE | 21

THE SHIFT | 25

THE TREATMENT | 31

THE VISITS | 37

THE BREAK DOWN | 41

THE CALL | 45

GETTING TO BETTER | 51

THE RECOVERY | 55

THE WALK | 59

THE SHUTDOWN | 63

TAKE YOUR REST | 67

AFTERWORD | 76

CHAPTER 1

IN THE BEGINNING

I was born Althea Angelique Barr on a Wednesday in August of 1969 at 5:48pm at Children's Hospital in Washington, D.C. I was born to William and Cathryn Barr, weighing seven pounds and five ounces and was the fourth of their four girls, and a sibling to my sisters, Felicia V. Barr, Vanessa L. Barr (Shang) and Annetta V. Barr (Bunny). My mother named me Althea after her close classmate and Angelique after someone on a television show.

I was born into a family of believers of Jesus Christ. My grandmother, Roxy Lamb, was a Missionary, and my grandfather, John Lamb, was an Elder at Bible Way's mother church in Washington, D.C.. Subsequently, my grandfather was ordained as a bishop, and Bishop John Lamb, would pastor True Way Bible Way Church and later, the Gospel Ark Temple Bible Way Church.

At one point in my grandfather's life, he was sick with tuberculosis (TB) and would remain in the hospital for three years. Another time he was sick was when his intestines ruptured, and the doctors and nurses did not think he was going to live. The story goes, the doctors stapled his stomach together and put him in the hall to die. The next day, his stomach popped open, and the nurse gave him a death needle. My grandfather said he prayed that God would keep him until the break of day, so when the nurse came to work that morning, she was shocked to see that he was still alive. God is always fighting for us.

My mother, Cathryn Lamb Barr, is the only girl out of six children. I was told she was a good child. She is such a kind and gentle soul because she was the only girl and she had all girls. I can truly say she is the best mother ever. She made it her mission to make sure that her girls understood that we are all we have and we are our own best friends. My sisters and I all have four very different personalities; yet, we are all super close.

My father, William Barr, was the second of many children born to Lillian Barr and Henry Alston. My father was from Richmond, VA and he moved to Washington, D.C. when he was about seventeen or eighteen years old. It's said that my father was his grandmother's favorite child. He used to travel with his grandmother all the time. She just knew my father was going to be a preacher. She started to call my father by the nickname, Joe, since Joe Louis was the heavyweight champion at the time.

My mother and my father met at Bible Way Church and were married by Bishop Smallwood E. Williams at Bible Way Church within a year. On my mother and father's first wedding anniversary, there was a big house fire at my father's mother's house in Richmond, VA that claimed the life of three of his very young siblings. The shock of losing three of his siblings did something to my father forever, and he was not as much of an emotional person after experiencing such a tragic loss.

Most of my father's family is still in Richmond, VA. We used to visit my father's side of the family in Richmond every summer. I loved spending time with my cousins as we all were pretty close. We had some really great times and some not so great times down there. I was a bad child and was very spoiled. I used to be a bully. I have had stitches in my head, my knee, my chin and my foot.

Overall, I must say that my childhood was pretty great. My dad made sure we did something every weekend. We would go crabbing and fishing, to the beach, to the drive-ins and to the movies. When we would go out, mom would often dress us alike. One time, my mom combed my sister Bunny and I's hair so pretty and dressed us alike before we went on a ferry ride. While we were on the ferry, a white lady who thought my sister and I were twins followed us all around the boat taking pictures of us. Many of my childhood experiences will be etched on my memory forever.

CHAPTER 2

THE NEIGHBORHOOD

My mom started working when I started school. I attended Park View Preschool and went on to attend Park View Elementary School. The principal's name was Mrs. Hayes and the Vice Principal's name was Mrs. Harper. I loved that school mainly because all the teachers already knew us because my older sisters had them so I was in good hands by the time I came along. The school felt like family until I got put out of school.

Our neighborhood was also like a family. Lamont Street is where I met my best friend and sister Denise Rollings and my little sis Daisy (Ms. Dee). We were very close. In the summertime, we stayed outside late playing games while all the adults who included my mom, Mrs. Alice, Mrs. Roberta's or Mrs. Minnnie would sit on the porch watching us. We grew up playing football with the guys and were all tomboys. They taught us how to be tough if we needed to be, so we definitely know how to fight and defend ourselves.

When my grandmother passed and granddad got remarried, we moved to 12th Street NW DC. At that time, it was the height of the heroin era. We lived right across the street from an empty parking lot. We saw people overdose on a regular. We would see women turning tricks, getting beat up and raped and people getting robbed. It was only by the grace of God that none of us got caught up in anything. We saw shoot outs and the jump outs arresting people all the time.

My parents made sure they kept us occupied. We had the big arcade games in our house, including Ms. Pac-Man, Pac-Man, Donkey Kong, all of them. My dad would cookout all the time. Our house was the hang out spot. My dad would take us to the MLK library and we would get all black history reels and black movies. On weekends, we would go to Ben's Chili Bowl. Every weekend, a man named Mr. Jack who lived next door to us would cook food and play movies for us in his closed in backyard. He would let us have birthday parties or just hang out. On 12th Street NW is where my sister Bunny met her husband Greg.

At the time, the city started working on the subway and out came the sewer rats. Those rats were big as cats. Our neighbor that lived across the street was outside with her dog one night and a rat attacked the dog. That had to be one of the craziest things I have ever seen.

By this time, I was graduating from Elementary school and started going to Shaw Jr. High School. I used to hang out at Uncle Red's place learning how to play pool; Uncle Red (Lawrence Thomas) had so many fish tanks in there. I knew everyone. I was the funny church girl. I kept everybody laughing all the time.

Due to having Scoliosis and back surgery, I was homeschooled for mid eighth grade and ninth grade, but I was able to graduate on time with my ninth grade class. I remember checking into the hospital and the person that checked me in was Patrick Ewing who at the time was still playing for Georgetown Hoyas. I was in the room with a white girl that was bulimic. She would drink water at weigh in right after a meal until the hospital staff got hip to what she was doing and started to lock the bathroom.

I stayed in the hospital for a week and I had to be in a body cast for six to eight months. Some of my friends would visit me on a regular, so I stayed connected. My sister Felicia had her son (T.J.) during that same time. He brought so much joy to the family. My dad finally had his son, and T.J. was the only boy in the family for thirty years until T.J. had his son.

I began my tenth grade year at Cardoza High School which was the same school my mom and dad had graduated from. That's where I met my first real boyfriend, Darnell. He was on the football team. That relationship was a very interesting experience. Need I say more.

CHAPTER 3

THE BIG MOVE

Our next move was to Bladensburg, Maryland; transitioning from a three bedroom home to a five bedroom home was a big change. Now, we all had our own bedroom. Our backyard was so huge, we hosted our family reunions at our house. My dad loved to have people over for cookouts.

I started high school at Bladenburg High School. Although we lived right across the street, I was late everyday. I hated that school. I had a few friends. There was this one teacher named Mr. Davis who was my History teacher. We used to talk a lot because he was a Christian. I wasn't a straight A student but I was a good student. I graduated high school on time.

After high school, I enrolled in Cosmetology school. I loved doing hair. I worked at a few salons and made good money. Then I started working at Macy's in downtown D.C. I really loved retail and meeting new people. I met a few well known people like President Jimmy Cater and his gracious wife for whom Macy's shut down the whole store while they shopped. Marvin Sapp was pleasant to talk with on more than one occasion. My favorite well known person was the legendary Edwin Hawkins who was surprised that someone recognized him at that time.

It was around this time, I found a lump on my right breast. The lump was so bad that it was sore to the touch. I went to the doctors at Howard Hospital. I think I was about twenty-four years old or so. The doctor came into the room, looked at me and then my chart and said, "You are too young to have cancer, stop eating chocolate". I was like, what! I demanded to see another doctor because I knew what I was feeling. I had to wait a few hours but the second doctor examined me and ordered tests and a biopsy, and it indeed was cancer, not the deadly kind but cancer. Thank God, they were able to get all of the cancer out. My sister Denise took me to my procedure. I remember not telling the rest of my family until after the procedure.

So fast forward, we moved to a house in Riverdale, Maryland which was right next to a Firehouse, but we never heard the firefighters leaving until they left out of the neighborhood. This house had five bedrooms and a huge backyard as well. We had parties, family reunions and cookouts all the time. We love to entertain.

I started working in Baltimore at Social Security Administration making Social Security cards, other important cards and mail. I think I was there for about five years. My nephew Cedric and I worked night shift. We loved it and we made some good money. I moved out into my own place. While working there, my feet and legs started to swell but I thought it was because I had to stand while I was working. My mother kept telling me to go see about it.

I went to the doctor and was told that my kidney level was dropping. A few months later, I had to stop working because the contract was up and I didn't make the cut on the new contract, so I moved back home after four years. I cried for months because I loved living alone. I later reunited with an old friend in North Carolina. I have known him since I was maybe fifteen or sixteen years old. I loved him then, and when we had a chance to talk again, I realized that I still loved him. I could tell that he may have felt the same way. We talked and laughed all night, then we decided that we would try to date again. In the beginning, it was rough because we argued all the time.

I did not realize I was sick and my body was going through changes. He was/is an amazing guy who is very patient, attentive and kind. We were together for nine years. While I thought we would have eventually been happily married, God had other plans for us. We will always be connected because our families are very close and my best friend married his brother. We are still friends. In fact, he has become my best friend.

CHAPTER 4

THE SHIFT

In March of 2013, my great nephew Caleb William Barr was on the way. We were very excited about the baby shower for him because he would be the first boy in the family in thirty years. The baby shower was planned for a Sunday. That Saturday, we asked dad to take us to a certain store, but he took us to a different store instead. While we were in the checkout line, he kept trying to give me his bank card. I should have known something was wrong because my dad doesn't give up any kind of money without a reason. He had been having mini strokes that whole weekend and we did not know it.

Dad was unusually quiet at the baby shower. On that Tuesday morning, dad got up and dressed for the day with his keys in his hand. Mom looked at him and said, "you don't look right in the eyes", so she took his keys and asked him, "where are you going?" and he said he didn't know. She then asked him, "what is your name?" and he didn't know it. She said, "well, who am I?" and he said, "I don't know". By that time, I was coming upstairs to go to work so mom asked, "who is that?" while pointing to me and he smiled and said, "I don't know".

It was at this point that I called my sisters, and we took dad to his doctor's office which was very close to the house. By the time we got there, the doctor told us to take him to the emergency room. While we were on the way to the hospital, Bunny turned the radio on and Jesus is Love was playing and dad, Bunny and myself started singing. He then asked Bunny for money to buy a chain saw to cut down some trees in the backyard.

When we got to the emergency room, they rushed dad to the back. When we finally got the chance to go to the back to see dad, he was completely out of it. Whatever question we asked him, his answer was, "Bishop James Silver". Dad loved Apostle Silver. When Apostle Silver used to call the house, he would ask to speak to the boss. Mom would say, "hold on, I have to go to the basement and untie him". They would laugh.

We would learn dad had a massive stroke. I think he stayed in the hospital for about three weeks. He was then sent to a rehab. When my sister heard the words "nursing home", she cried; she was so hurt thinking dad was going to stay there. Dad was in rehab about two months or so.

Dad had visitors every day. People would call to ask if they could go visit him. We always told them yes because, why not? Dad loved to talk. Sometimes, whoever was visiting him that day would take him for walks around the floor, go to physical therapy with him or even have lunch with him. They would also pray with dad's roommate. Everyone was kind to dad and us. One day, the nurse asked, "Who is this man? He must be someone important because he has visitors every day and lots of them". Throughout that whole ordeal, dad kept a smile on his face.

When dad came home, we celebrated. Dad taught us to celebrate everything because life is short and why not make someone else happy if you can. Dad was now functioning a little slower than normal due to having Aphasia, which is the loss of ability to understand and is caused by brain damage. Basically, dad would point to a cup and say, "shoe". Dad soon started going to speech therapy. We would go with him three times a week. The people there were so kind. Dad did really well. He and I would also go walking everyday.

In the meantime, I was being treated for Lupus. Lady Isabell Pollard would go to my appointments with me. Sometimes, she paid for some of my treatments and my medicine. She was such a blessing to me. This was before I had medical insurance. I'm so grateful that God placed good people in my life. During this time, I was on prednisone and had gained a lot of weight; I went from a size 10 to a size 18 within a year. I had gained so much weight that my feet were swollen and I couldn't fit any of my clothes or shoes.

Eventually, I started wearing my mom's dresses and slippers to church. The weight gain even caused me to start having to use a cane. I also recall an instance when my mom had to speak at the Mother church one week night. Of course, I went to the church service to support my mom. While I was at the service at the Mother church, my sister Vanessa had to go get a wheelchair for me because I had difficulty breathing.

After this incident happened, I visited my primary doctor who referred me to a specialist at Providence Hospital. Eventually, I was transferred from Providence Hospital to Washington Hospital Center to see a specialist. They found out I had Cirrhosis of the liver, which was caused by Hepatitis C. The doctors said I had a Mediterranean Strand, that I had as a child, probably from one of my many blood transfusions. Thankfully, Lady Pollard was there with me to ask the right questions on my behalf.

I remember I had to get my stomach drained and mom and Lady Pollard were there with me. I was lying in the hospital bed asking God, why me? Why am I going through this? Just as I asked the question , the lady on the other side of the curtain coded and they couldn't save her. I was like, okay God, I got it…

I also remember working at Macy's in downtown D.C. having to go up and down a ladder all day doing inventory. Dad came to pick me up from work that day. While walking to the car, I felt so tired and weak, partially because I was on my cycle. There were times when I stayed on my cycle for months at a time. Dad said that I looked pail so he dropped me off at the hospital. My hospital diet consisted of chocolate and ice. I loss weight and got a blood transfusion.

A few months later, I had to get a hysterectomy as a result of having fibroids for years. I was okay with getting one because I didn't want kids. After the procedure, I woke up to hearing my dad fussing about me being down in recovery for so long and how I needed to be in a room. My dad was a protector of his family in every possible way. He was definitely my hero.

CHAPTER 5

THE TREATMENT

My doctors started treating me for hepatitis C. I had to take this treatment, that was like chemotherapy but it was in pill form. It was horrible. I was in pain and sick all the time. I could not keep my food down and I slept a lot; but through it all, I kept going to church because I knew, one day, I would not be able to go. I was so sick at times, I would go to church and just lay on the back pew and fall asleep. I took the treatment for ten weeks, which was extended for another four weeks. God healed me of hepatitis C. I take blood work every three months and there has been no traces of hepatitis C. God does all things well.

After I had already started the process of getting health insurance, I was home one evening and I kept complaining that it was hard to breathe so my sister Vanessa took me to the emergency room. The hospital kept me that night and the case worker did the paperwork for insurance. I had so much fluid that I had to get my stomach drained. They put this huge needle in my stomach and pumped fluid out of me. A few days later, the doctor came to my room to tell me I needed a liver transplant. I was looking right at him the whole time but I didn't hear anything he said after liver transplant. I remember my sister Bunny, her daughter Shanice, Keith and his wife Kamaria being there but I don't remember who else was there. I recall Bunny and Shanice asking the doctor all types of questions. I was in shock and all kinds of thoughts were going through my mind. During every phase of my journey, God has always placed the right people in my life to ask the right questions for me.

One of the Bishops from Baltimore was trying to get me in Johns Hopkins Hospital. He said he had some connections there; I'm sure he did because he's well connected. Although I think Johns Hopkins Hospital accepts it now, I was contacted by them at a time when they were not accepting MedStar insurance so I was sent to Georgetown University Hospital because Washington Hospital Center had stopped doing transplants and Georgetown was their sister hospital.

Upon arriving at Georgetown University Hospital, I had to go through the evaluation process to qualify to be on the transplant list. This was an all day process. My mom and aunt Nita went with me. These two ladies have been a part of my support system every step of the way. When mom was home taking care of dad, she was unable to make some of my appointments but she was always there when she could be. Aunt Nita has stayed the night with me and changed my bed; she has been my eyes and ears to ask the right questions and has taken notes on everything. I believe I have a notebook regarding every appointment from the beginning up until now.

I think I was put on the Liver Transplant List in October of 2014. Meanwhile, my body was breaking down daily. In that following February, I went to Sunday morning service as usual and right at the end of service, I got really cold. I was sitting up front next to mom, which was right by the heating system and I couldn't get warm. There was an evening service that Sunday so I decided to go home because I was starting to feel bad, not sick, just bad. When I got home, I turned the heat on and up, put some pjs on, got in the bed and turned my blanket on. I still couldn't get warm; I was cold, cold. I had a doctor's appointment scheduled for the next day, so I thought I would be okay for the night.

By the time Aunt Nita and I got to the hospital for my appointment the next day, I was so weak. She asked if I needed a wheelchair and I told her no but I had really needed one. When we got to the doctor's office, the doctor looked at me and sent us down to the emergency room. I stayed in the hospital for two weeks. I cried every day during the second week. Basically, I had a mental breakdown. I had an infection but they couldn't figure out where it was coming from. They ran tests on everything to include my liver, my kidneys and my heart. My temperature kept going up and down and it took a few days to get my temperature to stay down.

It was discovered I had a cold sore, and the worse it got, the worse I got. I was treated for that and I still had a scar from that. I begged the doctor to send me home. I must have gotten on his nerves because he said, "Ms. Barr, I'm sending you home, you're not ready". I threatened to check myself out because someone really dear to me had passed away and I wanted to go to the service. I was home for two days and then right back in the hospital.

I had gone back in the hospital because I had started feeling different while I was sitting at the dining room table eating some fruit. I couldn't remember anything. My sister and her boyfriend helped me to my room to do my insulin. I remember getting the needle together and I don't remember anything else afterwards. I woke up in the emergency room to my mother's voice saying loudly, "she don't have AIDS, she was just tested. Why are y'all testing her again?" I couldn't open my eyes but I could still hear what was going on. I didn't know where I was but I knew I was alive. I finally opened my eyes, and I saw an Elder from the church. He began to ask me what happened, and I couldn't remember anything.

Aunt Nita sheds light on the occurrences of this time, noting, "I received a call that Angel needed to be rushed to the hospital. She was experiencing mental confusion. Larry and I rushed to the house, where Donny (a friend of the family) met us to help Larry carry Angel down two flights of icy outside stairs on a snowy day. Her body was full of fluid, making the task difficult for two strong men. We got her to the car, because the ambulance would have taken her to a different hospital and she had to go to Georgetown University Hospital. Larry drove us to the hospital where the hospital staff helped to get her out of the car and they rushed her to the emergency care unit. Within hours, the lobby was full of family members. Angel couldn't remember anything to include her name or her birthday. After treatment, she was back to herself".

CHAPTER 6

THE VISITS

It was now March 3, 2015 and I was at Georgetown University Hospital. I knew I was definitely going to be in the hospital for a while. I was still on the transplant list for my liver but I would now find out that my kidney had literally stopped working. I remember Elder Curtis Whitehead and another Elder came to visit me and he encouraged me to seek donors on my own. At this point, I only needed a piece of a liver because the liver rejuvenates itself. Oddly enough, I didn't want anyone I knew to be a donor, because in my mind, the first time I said no to that person, they would remind of the fact they saved my life.

My family came to see me every day while I was in the hospital. One time, I had to beg them not to come because it was snowing. The next day, I asked them again to not come up there because of the weather, and they came walking into the room a few hours later. My aunts Rosa Suber and Mary Nesbit came to sit with me during the week to give aunt Nita a break because aunt Nita's daughter, Sandra, was pregnant at that time and Sandra needed her mother.

On Saturdays, I had a visitor all day because my family and friends from far and near would come to visit me. I would look forward to Saturdays. One snowy Saturday, Bishop and Lady Demery came to visit me while I was still up walking. On another Saturday, my family brought my great nephew Caleb up to the hospital to see me. Caleb, who was about a year old was too young to come to my room, so I walked down the hall to the waiting room while I was still hooked up to an IV.

My sister Denise and her husband Darell would visit from Philadelphia. My nieces Denise and Dedria would spend the night with me sometimes. Denise would do my hair and my feet as I used to tell her to please make sure that my hair and my feet were taken care of. Vanessa would get in my bed with me all the time.

Sometimes on Sunday mornings, my aunt Tina would come sit with me for hours until my family came; then, she would go sit with her daughter because her daughter was pregnant at that time also. Sometimes, people I didn't know would visit me on the strength of my parents. This one Easter, a deacon from the Mother church was there visiting someone else and when he saw my parents leaving the hospital, he asked if he could visit me while he was there. I had no idea who that man was; he came to my room and said he knew my parents. This man sang about four or five songs, very loudly; in fact, he sang so loudly, the nurse kept asking him to lower his voice.

When the nurse came in to take my vitals, she asked if I wanted him to leave because she saw the expression on my face and I said, "yes, please". He was then asked to leave by the nurse. Easter was always a big deal for us. We would always have dinner at our house with lots of food, fun and plenty of love and laughter, so on this particular Easter, I was really missing everyone. Since there was always a lot of laughter in my room, how sick I was really never showed. Dad would pray for me every night before leaving the hospital. Sadness came at the end of the visits.

CHAPTER 7

THE BREAK DOWN

I was now getting weaker and weaker. I was loosing weight and I was not walking. I had about three IVs in my arms. I was not eating solid food because my body wasn't breaking it down anymore. I was going for different tests just about every day, sometimes a couple of times a day. When I had to go to another hospital to get some dental work done, I was transferred by ambulance to Washington Hospital Center. I was so happy to go outside.

Aunt Nita noted, "Angel had to get dental work done before the transplant. The purpose was to prevent possible infections. She was taken by ambulance. I met her at the other hospital and Angel, being the trooper she is, was smiling like she was on a fun ride. The doctor's concerns were that Angel would bleed out during the extractions, but by the Grace of God, she did not."

When I returned to my hospital room, I was bleeding. I had been bleeding for about a week, when I told the nurse to get me some warm salt water and I would be fine. She looked at me like I had three heads. I still didn't know I was as sick as I was. My family never let on how bad off I really was. Meanwhile, my body was shutting down.

I had to get a port in my neck for dialysis, which was one of the few times that I was scared. The port was put into my neck while I was in my room. The nurse laid me back flat in my bed. She numbed my neck and inserted the port. I had to go to dialysis twice a day. I would be taken down to dialysis at weird hours. I would fall asleep every time. I would say to myself, I'm going to stay up and see how the machine works. However, I would fall asleep every time. My skin became dark, ashy and flaky.

One day, I remember going down to dialysis and based on the looks on Vanessa and Bishop Demery's faces when they walked in, I thought to myself, I must really be sick. Only one person could stay with me so Vanessa left. When Bishop asked how I was doing and did I need anything, I covered my face and turned my back to him. He then began to pray, but the urgency in his voice was different. I remember him praying and asking God to touch and heal my body and put a rush on it. I didn't say anything, he stood there for a few minutes and left.

That particular evening, I remember being extremely weak and tired. In fact, I was so weak I couldn't keep my eyes open. I remember talking to everybody with my eyes closed. As it's told by my sister Felicia, the nurses asked everyone to leave so they could change me. While they were leaving, one said to the other, "we can't do anything else for her, we will just make her comfortable". My body was shutting down fast. I was bleeding from the inside. They took me off the transplant list because the nurse reported to the doctor that I was dying. I even had a stroke that evening.

My family came back in to say goodbye to me, not good night but goodbye. My sister's pastor, Pastor Parrish, came to pray for me. My dad came in to pray for me. I cried myself to sleep. For the first time, I felt like I was not going to wake up. My mom would always call when they got home, just to say good night again, so she called and we talked for a few minutes. After our call, I stayed up a while just thinking. I finally fell asleep, then about 3 or 4am I got the call…

My mom notes, "I remember standing at the foot of Angel's bed and praying to God to either heal her or take her. She was is so much pain. I hated to see my child lying there dying. I cried every night after leaving her. She was in bad shape; but God said, not yet, there is more".

CHAPTER 8

THE CALL

The doctor called and said, "Ms. Barr, we have a liver and kidney for you." When a person receives a transplant call, the doctor has to tell the person about the donor including if the donor has high blood pressure or diabetes and the potential recipient has the option to say yes or no. The person who is in need of a transplant is supposed to clearly say yes or no as the doctor has to hear the person say yes in order to proceed with a transplant.

I really didn't hear anything after the doctor said we have a liver and kidney for you. I started crying and said, "I need to call my mother." I continued crying while the doctor was telling me about my donor. Mind you, I was previously taken off the transplant list so I really wasn't even supposed to get that call; but God knows my end before my beginning. I believe God spoke up for me in that moment because I know I never verbally said the word, yes, to the doctor. I believe the doctor heard a yes although I never said yes. I'm a living witness that God will speak for you when you are speechless or don't know what or how to say something.

Aunt Nita notes, "When I got the call that Angel's transplant was about to take place, I believe it was early morning and still dark outside. Angel was so excited when the doctor told her, she didn't hear "it was going to happen in the morning." She made a call and everyone was at the hospital. We slept in the waiting room located on the same hospital floor where Angel was lying in her hospital bed. Some slept in chairs, and others on the floor. We were committed to waiting until she was ready to go into surgery. When Angel was taken into surgery, the family moved to the waiting area near where her eighteen to twenty hour surgery was taking place".

Vanessa notes, "I remember when we got the call about the surgery. Mom and dad were all packed and ready to leave for March Church Conference, when Angel called about the transplant happening on what I thought would be that morning. Everyone rushed up to the hospital. We were in the small waiting room because there were people in the bigger one, but we took over the bigger waiting room when those people left. I mean it was so many of us in that room. We were sleeping on the floor, on the chairs and everywhere. Carroll came down and brought hoagies for everyone and Denise and Darrell came down from Philadelphia. When I went up to Angels room to see what was taking so long, they were just rolling her down to pre-op. The nurse asked if I wanted to go with her, so I sat with her until they were ready for her surgery".

On the first day of the rest of my life, I remember the nurse coming in to prep me and give me something to relax me. While they were taking me down to pre-surgery, my sister Vanessa appeared. She had come to see what was taking so long and she came to my room just as they were rolling me out. The nurse asked if she wanted to sit with me until surgery began, so she sat with me. I remember I kept saying, "I wish they would hurry up". We sat for hours in the cold prep room.

The next thing I knew, I was waking up in my room in ICU. I had a breathing tube in my throat and I couldn't move because I was hooked up to the machines. What I thought was that same night was early the next day. When I woke up, the first thing the nurse did was remove the breathing tube. The first person I recognized was the Elder from the church asking me, "How do you feel about your new liver and kidney?" I said, "what kidney?" as I didn't remember anything about a new kidney.

I just started crying uncontrollably and they had to give me a needle to calm me down and I fell asleep.

I now had to wrap my mind around the fact that I had two new organs. I was a mess for a few days as that was all I could think about. That Sunday morning, I remember calling Carroll while he was at church. He was so happy to hear my voice and to know I was okay. The last time he had seen me was when I was in recovery.

After I woke up that same day, the nurse took me out of bed and sat me in the chair. When my family came in, I was sitting up in the chair. That was the first time I remember smiling in a long time. My medical team wasn't playing around and they had me start eating and drinking that same day. I hadn't had outside food in about a month and I was craving a Big Mac. It would be about another week before they let me eat one outside meal a day. Most of the time, I wanted my mom's cooking. During this time, I also started drinking coffee, because it was so cold I needed something warm to drink to warm me up.

Only my immediate family was able to visit me. I think I stayed in ICU for maybe two weeks. Of course, I had a pain pump but I never really used it other than sometimes at night to put me to sleep. When they moved me to another room, I was only allowed to go from the bed to the chair. I was a fall risk because I literally could not walk due to my body being all out of wack. It hurt to inhale and exhale.

I was told that my new organs came from an eighteen year old white girl from Baltimore. I think she, her dad and her uncle had gotten into a car accident while they were going to a baseball game. She and her dad had passed away. When I think about it, I still grieve for her family today. My family got to celebrate life renewed, but her family has to grieve the loss of two family members. I am not allowed to contact the family at all; the family has to contact me. Unfortunately, I can't even say, thank you, to her family.

CHAPTER 9

GETTING TO BETTER

It was now April and I had missed Caleb's second birthday. At one point, I thought I wouldn't be around to see him and Kristopher grow up. My god daughter Laila would ask Vanessa what was going on with me and why she couldn't talk to me. They eventually told her I was sick. Thankfully, I was able to FaceTime them whenever I would feel well enough.

Around this time, I started to become sicker. I couldn't even get out of the bed anymore. I couldn't feed, care for or do anything for myself. The nurse had to clean me up and feed me. The nurse would clean me up in the morning and my mom and my sisters would clean me up in the evening before I went to bed.

My red blood cells were going crazy. It felt like I had to have blood transfusions every week. At one point, I wasn't producing vitamin K so it was given to me through an IV. I had a bad reaction from the vitamin K IV and got dark spots all over my body. In my opinion, I looked like a leper.

Eventually, I started to get better and the doctor came to take the port out of my neck. That evening, another doctor came to take the three drain bags out. The way that doctor removed the bags almost felt like she snatched them out. My side was hurting so much. All the doctor said was, it will be okay in a few minutes. There was so much blood, more than I thought there should have been. Hours went by and I was still bleeding. The physical therapist came by to walk me around the unit, but I couldn't go because I was still bleeding. This is when they packed that area and put me back in bed.

Early the next morning about 3:00am, the nurse came to check my vitals. Because I was now use to needles, I just took my arms from underneath the covers. The nurse turned on the lights and screamed, "oh my God", which of course scared me. I opened my eyes and saw all this blood in my bed. I was rushed down to emergency surgery because whatever that doctor had done pulled something and I needed surgery again. I had to have another blood transfusion. I thank God because I could have just bled to death in my sleep. A few days went by and I became able to do physical therapy. I didn't know that the body can forget how to function so fast. I had to learn how to walk and feed myself again. I had to learn how to walk up and down steps and write my name and address again.

By this time, I was literally taking more than seventy different medications a day, and each medication had different side effects. I had the trembles, I couldn't remember things sometimes and I now weighed about 100 lbs. In my opinion, I looked horrible. Sometimes, my oxygen level would drop for no reason. I had to have a breathing tube in my nose all the time. My night nurse would give me popsicles. Thankfully, I got to the point I was eating enough to go home so mom and I took a class on post surgery home care. I went home on May 3rd, which is notable because I was admitted on March 3rd. I also find noteworthy, my birthday is August 24th, my surgery date was March 24th and my dad passed on September 24th.

When uncle Bishop and aunt Nita took me home, uncle Bishop kept asking me, did I know how to get home. I couldn't remember anything including people sometimes. When we pulled up at the house, the look on my dad's face was priceless. He came down the steps to greet me and help me into the house. He was on my left side with his arm around my right side. He was squeezing me so tight that I had to change my bandages when I got in the house. When I got in my bed, it felt like I was lying in the arms of Jesus. I have the most comfortable bed ever.

CHAPTER 10

THE RECOVERY

I was now home where the real work began. At this time, I weighed about 98 lbs. l had doctor's appointments every week. I had physical therapy three times a week and a home care nurse would come to assist me three times a week. I was walking with a walker. I was constantly losing weight. I was in so much pain because being that small, it was hard for me to walk, sit and lay. I was fighting depression every day as I had to have someone to clean me up, to bathe me and I couldn't do anything for myself. I couldn't travel or be around animals for five years. I couldn't get life insurance for six years because the body most likely goes into rejection of the new organs within the first six years.

I had to take a total of seventy pills a day - morning, noon and night. My body was going though all kinds of changes. l wasn't really sleeping or eating. For a few months, my weight fluctuated between 96 pounds and 100 pounds. I was nothing but skin and bones. I had a doctor's appointment every week. The doctor put me on a medication often given to AIDS patients to prompt them to gain weight. The doctor said if the medication didn't work, the next step would be to try a feeding tube. Thank God, the medication started to work. All my hair fell out, which was devastating. I remember Carroll telling me, "okay babe, you have 24 hours to cry and then get yourself together. You have already been through the hard part, your hair will grow back". Vanessa said, "we're going to go through this together", and she shaved her head so I would feel better.

I slowly started gaining weight again. At first, physical therapy was a challenge because depression had set in. It was hard not being able to do anything for myself. My family and friends were very supportive. I remember my goddaughter's mother Moneta coming to see me and the hug she gave me was just what I needed. I had plenty of help with rides to my appointments (Tina, Jon-Jon, aunt Nita, my nieces and sisters) and I was able to get Metro Access to travel on my own.

I remember looking in the mirror one day and noticing my eyes being so white and clear. My skin had a beautiful tone. I loved my short hair. For the first time in a long time, I saw the beauty in me. I understood that what I was going through was not just for me but others needed to see a modern day miracle. I realized I was worth fighting for and I was alive because there's more.

When I went to my one year doctor's appointments, all of my doctors surprised me. My doctors were happy with my progress. My kidney doctor said to me, "Ms. Barr, we really worked hard for you. I had to take your liver out in pieces. When we opened you up to remove it, it crumbled into pieces because it was completely dead". I began to cry while he was talking and so did some of them. I still go back to Georgetown University Hospital for my once a year check ups.

To celebrate my one year anniversary celebration, I rented an event hall called E & J Event Center. During my journey, I experienced people telling me all kinds of foolishness including a lady who told me God showed her I had a big black snake in my stomach. Therefore, I only wanted the people who supported me during my journey to attend my celebration.

My one year celebration was everything I dreamed it would be. There were only about fifty people there. I had all the people that I love there. My aunt Tina and her team prepared the food and my sister Bunny gifted my cake and cupcakes. My colors were green and white. My sister and her family came down from Philadelphia and Carroll and one of his sisters came down. I had a praise dancer to perform and a few speakers. There was a little music, a little dancing and lots of laughs and love. I remember speaking at the end and while I was looking out at everyone, I was thinking how grateful I was to be alive.

CHAPTER 11

THE WALK

While I was getting better, dad was having more challenges. Dad, Caleb and I would walk around the block or to the corner store every day. When we started letting dad walk around the block by himself, he did great at first. Then about a month later, we let him walk around the block as usual and he didn't come back. I went out alone to look for him and when I didn't find him after about ten minutes, I called my sisters and everyone with a car to come to the house.

In the meantime, I went back out to search in another direction. I called Carroll who began to pray once I started crying while we were on the phone. When I returned to the house, it was only a few minutes later when a police car pulled up with dad in the back seat. Mom always kept dad's ID in his pocket so someone would know where to take him. The police found him about ten minutes away sitting on the steps of a church. We took him to the hospital and found out that he had suffered another stroke. This time, he stayed in the hospital about a week.

During this same time, my sister Vanessa (Shang) had a stroke. I took dad to a funeral at the Mother church and while there, I received three missed calls from my sister Bunny which was very unsettling because she normally communicated with me by text. When I called her back, she said, "Shang had a stroke and is at the hospital". I met Bunny at the hospital. Now, mom was taking care of dad and I was taking care of Shang. Fortunately, Shang started physical therapy and began getting better.

The doctor told us if a person has a stroke under the age of sixty, it's hereditary and that my sisters and I are likely to have one. As I'm writing the book, my oldest sister Felicia had a stroke and is doing good and back at work and I had one as well and didn't even know it. One year later on the exact same day, Vanessa had another stroke. By the mercies of God, everything the enemy tried didn't work. Through all of this, mom and dad were still pastoring. We had plenty of help, thanks to Apostle Silver and by this time, Bishop Demery sent Elders to support us at the church. Eventually, mom decided to retire dad because his health was not improving. We had a big retirement service and we joined the Mother church under the leadership of Bishop and Lady Demery.

Life was great again as mom and dad could rest and relax, Vanessa had recovered and was back at work and I was doing great. Then, dad was diagnosed with Parkinson's disease and dementia. While we had kind of figured this was the case, it hit different when we heard dad's actual diagnosis. Dad began to get slower and slower.

CHAPTER 12

THE SHUTDOWN

When the Pandemic hit, everything shut down. Everyone was wearing masks. We had stopped hugging and shaking hands. I had always wore masks during cold and flu season, and when I did, people at church would laugh at me and say hurtful things sometimes. Now, everyone had to wear masks so they were asking me where I got my masks from.

During this time, my anxiety was through the roof. Even before the shutdown, I hadn't gone outside for about three months. Because of my transplants, I thought in my mind, I would die if I got COVID-19. Due to how overwhelmingly afraid I was, my doctor had to put me on medication. I didn't like the way the medication made me feel so I stopped taking them.

One night during the pandemic, the Lord spoke to me in a dream. In the dream, I had a business making body scrubs and beauty products. When

I woke from the dream, I started doing research and about a month or so later, I started my own business. I am now an Entrepreneur with a LLC, "Roxy J Scents".

About four months into the pandemic, mom, dad and I all tested positive for COVID. I was devastated. At first, we weren't having any symptoms. Mom and I did not have a fever, cough or anything. Days went by and mom and I started experiencing symptoms. Dad was now non-verbal so we didn't know how he was feeling. Then, dad stopped eating.

One particular night, dad was so weak that mom and Shang had to help him walk to his bed. As soon as they got him into the bed, he passed out. We called the paramedics. When the paramedics came, they tested his sugar and it was 528. They took him to the hospital and kept him about a week or so. That was very difficult for us, because we couldn't visit him. His nurse was a member of our church and she was a Godsend. She would send us pictures and FaceTime us to let us see dad.

When dad came home, I had welcome home yard signs and balloons out front. We were so excited to see him. We had taken down the dining room table and turned the dining room into a bedroom for him. We ordered a hospital bed that was set up real nice and comfortable for him. He was able to see the TV from there. He was still walking; he struggled but was still walking. We got him a wheelchair. He hated the wheelchair and was always trying to get out of it so we had to start strapping him in it. One day when mom and I were doing our daily tasks around the house, I walked through the living room and there was dad standing at the front door while being strapped to the wheelchair. I yelled for mom and we laughed. Dad turned around to look at us with the biggest smile on his face. Then, we all laughed some more. I don't know why I didn't take pictures.

Dad taught us to find laughter in anything. He was so funny and he was great with people. I think I got my people skills from him. He could enter a room in which he didn't know anyone, and by the time he made his rounds, everyone knew who he was and loved him. When we would be out, people would stop to talk to dad and he would ask about their families. We would ask dad, "who was that?", and he would say, "I don't know the person from a can of paint". Like my dad, I love meeting new people. My family always says I missed my calling and I should be a comedian. I can find the humor in anything. The downside of being the life of the party, is who's there to make me happy. Most of the time when I'm down, I have to push how I'm feeling aside to make everyone else laugh. I am always expected to be happy and light. It can get very exhausting. Nevertheless, it's become a part of who I am.

CHAPTER 13

TAKE YOUR REST

It felt like we were taking dad to a different doctor every week. Mom would get dad up for breakfast and he would usually be sitting down while he waited for her to get the wheelchair, but on this one particular day, he felt like walking and he fell. I went to help him up and he made a sound I had never heard before, so I knew he was injured. I sat him in his chair, then moved him to the sofa. I knew he had broken his hip because he couldn't walk. I called my sisters and everyone to tell them dad had fallen and broken his hip. The paramedics came and took him to the hospital. This happened on Mother's Day weekend and dad had a hip replacement on Mother's Day.

Dad was then sent to a rehab/nursing home which was the worst decision we could have made. That decision was the beginning of the end. That nursing home was slowly killing him. It was right in the middle of the pandemic so we couldn't visit him for two weeks. That was heartbreaking because he probably thought we left him there forever. We would have to make appointments to see dad. After two weeks, Bishop Demery was able to get the first appointment, so we were like, okay, good. Bishop Demery was able to visit dad for a full hour and he sent us pictures. Bishop Demery told us that dad remembered him. Bishop Demery was a true blessing through the whole ordeal. We could tell by the pictures that dad was losing weight. By the time mom and I finally got to see him, he looked disoriented and very thin. We asked a lot of questions. They told us that dad was doing good.

When dad first went to the nursing home, we sent clothes and I made a big picture board with pictures of the family and people he would recognize. When my sisters visited him, dad had on dirty clothes and did not have any socks on. If you know the Barr girls, we don't play when it comes to our family so they heard about that and everything else we felt was unacceptable. The next day, dad had a doctor's appointment at the hospital and we met him there. He came with a nurse aid and she was very kind to him. After the appointment, the nursing home hadn't scheduled dad a way home, so we waited five hours for a ride to come. About a week after that, dad had another doctor's appointment and the nursing home sent him alone with an envelope for public transportation.

I was livid; I called the nursing home and let them have all of it. How dare they send a non-verbal person alone on public transportation. If we hadn't been there to meet him, anything could have happened.

Not long after that, mom received a call that dad had stop eating but there was no need for us to come up there, they just wanted mom to know. Mom went in her room, I went on the porch and we were both praying and crying. We met in the living room and said at the same time, "let's go". Of course, I called my sisters and they met mom and I there. Due to the pandemic, we couldn't just walk in and check on him. The nursing home wouldn't let mom go back to see him, so after going back and forth with them, mom said, "call the ambulance, we're taking him out of here".

When the ambulance took dad out of the nursing home, he looked dead. They got him to the hospital and took him in the back. When mom and I got in the back to see him, dad was barely breathing. It was bad so mom told me to call the family and Bishop Demery. The doctor told us that dad was basically being starved and dehydrated. The only time they took him out of bed was when he had visitors. He couldn't talk so he couldn't tell us what was happening to him. He had nasty bed sores. The only time he was eating was when we took him food. Mom would cook and take it to him, but because we couldn't see him every day, he wasn't eating every day.

The doctors at the hospital were kind and very gentle with dad. He stayed on IV feeding for about three weeks. He started gaining weight and smiling again. He started doing physical therapy and began walking again and sitting up on the side of the bed. He then got an infection and the Parkinson's disease started to run its course. It became difficult for him to swallow. They put a feeding tube through his nose but after a couple days of that, dad snatched it out. Only family and clergy were able to visit him. His body was now breaking down. Dad had a feeding tube put in surgically. I then began to make arrangements to have another hospital bed and feeding supplies delivered to the house. We had to learn how to feed him and clean the tubes.

When dad came home, we celebrated. Mom and I had a routine. We would get him up at 8:00am to clean and change him before his 9:00am feeding. His second feeding was at noon, his third feeding was at 3:00pm and his last feeding was at 6:00pm. We changed him and gave him his medication in between his feedings. Vanessa would sleep in his room at night and I would sit with him until 8:00am. On weekends, dad had many visitors from in and out of town, to include his family from Richmond and his family from Philadelphia, who would come down to love on him.

It was now August when dad and I always celebrated our birthdays together. It was always a great celebration. One evening that August, dad began to have a fever and it started to get worse and worse. We called the hospice nurse and she came to the house. She told us to put cool, wet towels on him to help bring his fever down. She said the fever was a result of the inscision from the hip replacement which had become infected and dad was now transitioning. She informed us that dad had about three days left to live. I called the family and the people he loved. He had so many visitors. For three days, my sisters stayed at the house every night.

On the night dad passed away, his children, grandchildren, great-grand son and godchildren were present. No random people were present, just family. I had just fed dad and my sisters Bunny and Felicia began changing him. They had turned him over and when they turned him back around, his breathing was labored. Bunny yelled for me to come check him. I checked his pressure and oxygen and they were very low. For the last three days, I had checked his vitals every hour. Everyone came in the room and stood around the bed and he passed away about five minutes later. It was very peaceful. He passed away just the way he would have wanted it. Mom got in bed with him and that broke my heart.

Everyone had their time with dad. I couldn't cry, I just kissed him. I felt empty and lost, but in true Angel fashion, I had to make sure everyone else was okay. My nephew Kaden, who was maybe three or four years old, kept going into the room to look at Pop. I finally asked Kaden, was he okay, and he said he was sad because Pop was dead and I said, "it's okay because Pop is with Jesus". He said, "oh okay", and went back outside; a few minutes later, he came back in, went into Pop's room, climbed in the chair that was right beside his bed and just looked at Pop. We had to wait for the hospice nurse to come to clean dad up and to call the time. She had to watch me flush all his pain medication and I had to sign some paperwork. At about 9:00pm, the funeral home came to pick up his body.

When it was time to plan the service, our pastor, Bishop Demery, was there for us every step of the way. He and Elder Simon were a huge help to us. Mom said she didn't want to do anything and that the girls could do it all. We each had a job to do and we all got our jobs done. We didn't get in each other's way while we did our jobs. We went to view the body the night before his service and he looked great. Everyone was crying but I still couldn't cry; we still had some things to do.

On the morning of the service, we got to the church and I was still in "I still have things to do mode". I was trying to keep certain people away from mom because people can say some crazy things sometimes. When it was time to line up and walk in, I was walking in with Carroll while thinking, there's nothing for me to do. I became a mess. I was crying and shaking. I walked up to the casket for the last viewing and to close the casket.

I could not put my hands on that casket. I had to stand there and say goodbye to my dad forever. I just couldn't wrap my head around the fact that he was gone forever. After my sisters closed that casket, my body felt like a ton. I laid across the casket totally broken. That day took something out of me forever. Being at the cemetery was just as bad because it was final. Looking at that casket for the final time was heartbreaking all over again.

We had a repast the next day which gave us time to process the fact that dad was gone. The repast was great; it was just for family and close friends and there was a big fight that was coming on TV that night. We have always been a sports family, especially football and boxing. Having all girls, dad could care less about sports. He rooted for whoever was winning. I remember Bishop Eric Cater, his wife and daughter Mia came to the repast and Bishop Cater stayed to watch the fight with us that night and that meant so much to us. The house was now quiet, the dining room was put back together and now I had to figure out what my new normal would be. I had to find a way to live. I had to now figure out a way how to not get stuck in grief and depression. I had to remember that this is what dad preached about and lived for…To Live Again.

EPILOGUE

Ultimately, this is the memoir of my journey to becoming me. You may ask the question, "who are you?" I am a strong, smart, talented, beautiful, confident black woman who has finally become comfortable in her own skin. I am Althea Angelique Barr and I still believe.

AFTERWORD

Things had to get worse, things had to look bad, for God to show how great He is and how merciful He is. We all can say God is great and He's greatly to be praised, but there are only a few who can really say GOD IS TRULY A GREAT GOD.

God creates situations in order to reveal Himself to us. He created a situation for revelation and He called it, Jehovah Nissi - The Lord is my banner. He created a situation for revelation and He called it, Jehovah Rapha - The Lord that Healeth. God had an appointed time for Angel's release, and I thank God for her healing.

It was now March 24th, 2016. After Angel's surgery, my brother Darrell and sister Denise were already down in Washington, D.C. at the hospital in the waiting room along with Shang, mom and dad. Shorty thereafter, my brother called to give me an update. After hearing the news, I stopped what I was doing, gathered myself and drove down that Tuesday afternoon. When I arrived at the hospital, I saw Bishop Barr, Lady Cathryn, Shang, Denise and my brother there in the waiting area.

My brother and I went back to the recovery room while Angel was lying there sedated from several hours of surgery. We talked briefly with the nurse and then went back to the waiting area. It seemed as if hours passed by as we were talking in the waiting room. We were all about to leave when Bishop Barr and I went back to the recovery room. When we walked into the room and stood on opposite sides of Angel's bed, Bishop looked up and said to me, "Pray son". As Bishop stood on one side of the bed and I stood on the other side, Bishop reached down and touched Angel's body while I reached out, touched her hand and prayed a prayer of thanksgiving.

I'll never forget the sound that came from Bishop's mouth that only a grateful parent can ever utter. As I prayed, Bishop said, "THANK YOU!" with a voice that pierced my soul. Bishop was so sincere in not asking God for anything but with a heart of THANKSGIVING, he kept saying, "THANK YOU, THANK YOU, THANK YOU!!", over and over again.

For all that God had done in Bishop's life, this one was something he could never thank Him enough for. When you love someone, you feel their pain, you feel their hurt, you feel their uncertainties, but when you KNOW God, you have an advantage.

Even on this very day, I too say, "God, I Thank You!". On March 24th, God said to Angel, "It's time for your healing and the birth of your miracle". Let me say this - there is no sound sweeter than when God says, "It's Time".

I don't know who I'm talking to today, but God had appointed a day for Angel's release. I came all the way from Philadelphia to tell her - THIS DAY, IS THE DAY, WHEN GOD SAID - "IT'S TIME!!!!"

With so much sickness and things looking so dim, some of us would've given up, but God had a plan already worked out. God said - "IT'S TIME!" He created a situation for revelation.

~ Carroll W. Gibbs

AFTERWORD

I have known Angel for well over 40 years. The warm, positive and generous lady that you will come to appreciate through "Worth Fighting For" will not only encourage you to face life's challenges, but will also add to your level of faith. Angel has approached each day with a smile, high energy and hard work. She does not simply talk the talk - she walks the walk!

Upon reading this book, I discovered a personal initiate journey of a fighter. It reminds me of the adage that everyone has a story to tell. Her story of overcoming difficulties and not allowing circumstances to dictate your outlook on life is a must read for both young and old. This book is not just another religious story, but gives practical insights into how to navigate various storms of life. Angel put a real face on the description of a fighter!!

I hope this book is widely circulated and taken to heart not only by Christians, but even more importantly by those who may find themselves in a battle. Then I believe they will share in the possibility that Life is Worth Fighting For!!

~ Bishop M.K. Smith

AFTERWORD

Angelique Barr has placed us on the front row of her life's journey. What more can I say about the foundational tenets of faith to triumph and the unwavering desire to rise to the challenge. The mental fortitude alone to endure what this woman of God has is absolutely exceptional. She is the prime example of who the Apostle Paul talks about, when he says in 1 Timothy 6:12, expressing that we should "fight the good fight of faith."

To be as resolute and determined regardless of her medical diagnosis and future forecast are the things that testify to faith and how faith works - to believe, to receive then to conceive that which you stand upon, immovable always abounding.

Angelique is a living and teaching demonstration of what victory looks like. The victorious must endure a conflict in order to rejoice when the battle is won. May we all experience growth by hearing her story, knowing that just one chapter from your story can impact someone else's life positively. As overcomers we can use these testimonies to help us overcome individually and collectively.

"And they overcame him by the blood of the Lamb, and by the word of their testimony...." Revelation 12:11

Thank you Angelique Barr, for by your overcoming, you are helping us overcome.

~ Elder Lewis Johnson Jr.

For booking and contact, email
Angel082469@yahoo.com

Made in the USA
Middletown, DE
08 March 2025